Macroeconomics

Fourth Edition *UPDATE*
2002–2003

Andrew B. Abel
The Wharton School of the
University of Pennsylvania

Ben S. Bernanke
Woodrow Wilson School of
Public and International Affairs
Princeton University

Addison
Wesley

Boston   San Francisco   New York
London   Toronto   Sydney   Tokyo   Singapore   Madrid
Mexico City   Munich   Paris   Cape Town   Hong Kong   Montreal

Editor-in-Chief:	Denise Clinton
Executive Development Manager and Development Editor:	Sylvia Mallory
Marketing Manager:	Adrienne D'Ambrosio
Managing Editor:	James Rigney
Production Supervisor:	Katherine Watson
Design Manager:	Regina Kolenda
Senior Media Producer:	Melissa Honig
Text Design, Electronic Composition, and Project Management:	Elm Street Publishing Services, Inc.
Cover Designer:	Joyce Cosentino Wells
Manufacturing Supervisor:	Hugh Crawford
Printer:	R. R. Donnelley and Sons

Library of Congress Cataloging-in-Publication Data

Abel, Andrew B., 1952–
    Macroeconomics / Andrew B. Abel, Ben S. Bernanke. —4th ed. update
       p. cm.
    Includes index.
    ISBN 0-321-12228-3
      1. Macroeconomics.   2. United States—Economic conditions.
I. Bernanke, Ben. II. Title.
HB172.5.A24   2003
339—dc21   00-038105

Contents

Introduction v

Chapter 2 *UPDATE* Surprise, Surprise! Fourth-Quarter 2001 GDP Figures Defy Expectations 1

Chapter 4 *UPDATE* A Ricardian Tax Cut? 3

Chapter 4 *UPDATE* Macroeconomic Consequences of the Boom and Bust in Stock Prices 5

Chapter 6 *UPDATE* A U.S. Productivity Miracle? 8

Chapter 7 *UPDATE* U.S. Monetary Aggregates, 2002 10

Chapter 8 *UPDATE* Dating the Peak of the 2001 Recession 11

Chapter 11 *UPDATE* Efficiency Wages in the Laboratory: Testing Akerlof's Gift-Exchange Theory 14

Chapter 13 *UPDATE* The Weakness of the Euro 17

Chapter 13 *UPDATE* Crisis in Argentina 20

Chapter 14 *UPDATE* The Federal Reserve Responds to the Recession 23

Chapter 14 *UPDATE* Game Theory Goes to the Oscars 25

Introduction

This *UPDATE* to *Macroeconomics,* Fourth Edition, provides substantial new material for students and instructors using the text. Our emphasis in the *UPDATE* is on developments in the U.S. and world economies during the past year, including the recession that began in March 2001, consequences of the boom and bust in U.S. stock prices, effects of the 2001 tax rebates, recent developments in U.S. productivity growth, causes and effects of the Argentine crisis, and the last stage in the introduction of the euro.

UPDATEs are arranged in parallel to the text, with specific page and chapter references to the Fourth Edition, permitting easy integration into the course. *UPDATEs* do not introduce new analytical material but rather apply ideas from the text. Students should thus be able to tackle these readings on their own, even if time does not permit full discussion in class.

PowerPoint slides of the figures and tables in this *UPDATE* are available on the textbook's companion Web site, www.aw.com/abel_bernanke.

A.B.A.
B.S.B.

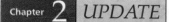

Surprise, Surprise! Fourth-Quarter 2001 GDP Figures Defy Expectations

In November 2001, the National Bureau of Economic Research (NBER), the non-profit organization that is the semi-official arbiter of recessions and booms, declared that a recession had begun in the United States in March of that year (see Chapter 8 *UPDATE*). The manufacturing sector weakened in the fall of 2000, and the NBER determined that the slowdown had spread to the broader economy by March 2001, the month in which economywide employment began to fall. The economic disruptions following the September 11, 2001, terrorist attacks worsened the economic downturn. During the two months following September 11, the unemployment rate increased by 0.6 percentage points, and the short-term economic outlook was very gloomy. In November, the Federal Reserve Bank of Philadelphia's regular survey of the view of professional forecasters found that the forecasters were predicting that real GDP would fall at a 1.9% annual rate during the fourth quarter of 2001. But within four months of this pessimistic projection, the Bureau of Economic Analysis (BEA) surprised economy watchers with three pieces of unexpected good news about GDP growth in the fourth quarter.

The BEA regularly releases three successive estimates of quarterly GDP. *Advance* estimates are released about one month after the end of the quarter; *preliminary* estimates are released about two months after the end of the quarter; and *final* estimates are released about three months after the end of the quarter. The *advance* estimates for fourth-quarter 2001 GDP growth, released January 30, 2002, revealed an unexpected but pleasant development. According to these early estimates, rather than falling as widely predicted, real GDP actually grew at the small but positive annual rate of 0.2% during the fourth quarter of 2001. The primary factors contributing to this growth, according to the advance estimates, were a 5.4% annualized growth in personal consumption expenditures and a 9.2% annualized growth in government purchases. The main source of increased consumption spending, in turn, was expenditure on consumer durable goods, which grew at an annualized rate of 38.4%! The strong growth in durable goods expenditure primarily reflected healthy automobile sales, which were stimulated by aggressive rebate offers and zero percent financing deals by car manufacturers. Increased government spending on security and military preparedness following the terrorist attacks also contributed to a higher real GDP. On the other hand, investment spending declined sharply, at an annual rate of 23.7%, during the fourth quarter.

A month later, the February 28, 2002, release of *preliminary* estimates contained a second pleasant surprise: According to these more complete data, real GDP had grown at an annual rate of 1.4% during the fourth quarter of 2001. That is, the estimate of real GDP growth was revised upward by 1.2 percentage points, which is more than double the typical size of a revision between the advance and preliminary estimates.

Consumer spending that was even stronger than previously reported, together with a higher figure for U.S. exports, accounted for most of the upward revision.

The March 28, 2002, *final* estimates delivered yet a third pleasant surprise, with the report that real GDP grew at an annual rate of 1.7% during the fourth quarter of 2001. An increased estimate of net exports of services was the major factor contributing to the 0.3 percentage point revision above the preliminary estimates. In short, after three rounds of estimates, the fourth quarter of 2001 appears now to have been a period of modest growth rather than sharp contraction.

The surprisingly high estimates of fourth-quarter GDP growth led some to question whether a full-fledged recession had begun in 2001 after all. A common rule of thumb is that a recession corresponds to two consecutive quarters of falling real GDP. Although real GDP fell in the third quarter of 2001, the finding that it actually rose during the fourth quarter means that the economic weakness of 2001 would not qualify as a recession, according to this rule of thumb.

The NBER, however, rejects the "two-negative-quarter" rule-of-thumb definition of a recession, for two main reasons. First, the NBER economists prefer not to rely on the behavior of a single economic variable, even one as important as real GDP, to define a recession. They pointed out, for example, that employment had decreased substantially during 2001, as happens during a typical recession. It was only because output per worker—which usually declines during recessions—grew at the surprisingly high annual rate of 5.1% in the fourth quarter of 2001 that total real GDP was able to increase, despite continuing declines in employment. Taking labor market developments into account as well as real GDP, the NBER still viewed the episode as a recession. A second reason for not relying strictly on real GDP for determining whether the economy is in recession is that GDP figures can be quite substantially revised over time—as the experience of 2001 shows clearly! Thus one would not want to rely on GDP figures alone in making judgments about the state of the economy.

A Ricardian Tax Cut?

I n May 2001, Congress passed, and President Bush signed, the Economic Growth and Tax Relief Reconciliation Act of 2001, which featured both short-run and long-run tax cuts. In the short run, and in response to concerns about the ongoing economic slowdown, the Act included a provision for the distribution of rebate checks to taxpayers. To be mailed out over a period of months beginning in July 2001, the rebates were as large as $300 for an individual, $500 for a head of household, and $600 for a married couple. The longer-run tax cut provided by the Act decreased income tax rates. For couples filing a joint return, the tax rate on the first $12,000 of income was reduced from 15% to 10%. The highest tax rate, paid by upper-income taxpayers, was to be reduced to 35% from 39.6% over a five-year period, and other tax rates would be reduced by 3 percentage points over a five-year period.

Largely as a result of this tax bill, Federal receipts in the third quarter of 2001 were $180.3 billion (seasonally adjusted at annual rates) lower than in the first quarter of that year. If the Ricardian equivalence proposition (p. 123 of the Fourth Edition) holds, then a tax cut should have no effect on consumption or national saving. Specifically, although a tax cut reduces government saving by reducing the budget surplus, Ricardian equivalence suggests that the tax cut should increase private saving by an equal amount, leaving national saving (the sum of government saving and private saving) unchanged.

Table 1 compares various components of national saving in the first quarter of 2001, before the tax cut was enacted, and in the third quarter of 2001, after taxpayers had begun to receive rebates and to benefit from reductions in tax rates. The results appear to fit the predictions of the Ricardian equivalence proposition. Government saving fell by $228.5 billion (at an annual rate) from the first quarter

Table 1

Ricardian Equivalence and the Tax Cut of May 2001

	2001:Q1	2001:Q3	Change
	billions of dollars (seasonally adjusted at annual rates)		
Private saving	1307.9	1534.4	226.5
Personal	78.8	285.3	206.5
Business	1229.1	1249.1	20.0
Government saving	446.1	217.6	-228.5
Federal	303.7	86.2	-217.5
State and local	142.5	131.4	-11.1
National saving	1754.0	1752.0	-2.0

Note: Numbers may not add to totals due to rounding.
Source: Survey of Current Business, February 2002, Table 5.1, D-14.

to the third quarter of 2001, reflecting the losses in tax revenue. But during this time period, private saving increased by an almost identical $226.5 billion, so that national saving in the third quarter was virtually identical to its value in the first quarter. Effectively, the public chose to save virtually all of the tax cut, at least in the short run, so that consumption and national saving did not change. (Remember, Ricardian equivalence applies to changes in taxes or transfers but not to changes in government saving that arise from changes in government purchases. In this episode, the overwhelming proportion of the change in government saving stemmed from reduced taxes and increased transfer payments.)

There is some evidence that by early 2002 consumers had begun to spend out of their tax rebates, a trend weakening the case for pure Ricardian equivalence. Nevertheless, this episode illustrates that fiscal policymakers face a difficult challenge in predicting exactly how consumers will react to a given change in taxes or transfers.

Macroeconomic Consequences of the Boom and Bust in Stock Prices

S tock prices in the United States soared during the 1990s, especially during the second half of the decade, but then tumbled sharply early in the first year of the new century. Illustrating these trends, Figure 1 shows two major stock price indexes. The Standard and Poor's (S&P) 500 is an index of 500 stocks representing a broad cross-section of corporations headquartered in the United States. The NASDAQ index, a newer index than the S&P 500 and one more oriented to smaller, startup firms, more closely reflects the behavior of stocks of firms in the technology sector of the economy. As you can see in Figure 1, in a little more than five years, from the end of 1994 until March 2000, the S&P 500 index increased dramatically in value, by a factor of 3.3. Even more spectacular was the rise in the NASDAQ index, whose value increased by a factor of 6.7 over the same period. (In other words, a dollar's worth of stock purchased on the NASDAQ at the end of 1994 would have been worth on average about $6.70 in early 2000, not including any dividends received.) Indeed, during the year ending in March 2000, the NASDAQ index more than doubled. The much larger increase in the NASDAQ

Figure 1
Stock prices in the United States
Sources: www.nasdaq.com and www.standardandpoors.com

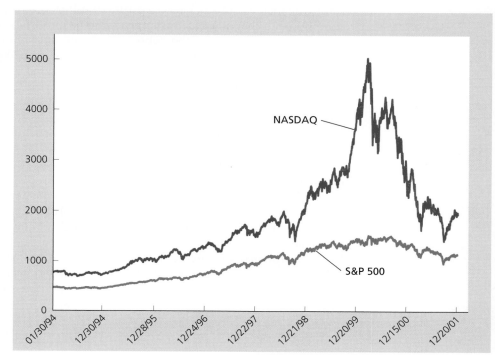

index than in the S&P 500 index reflected an intense demand for stocks in the technology sector as financial investors rushed to get a share of the "new economy" and the "dot-com revolution."

During the stock market's rise in the 1990s, many economists began to worry that firms' stock prices were too high to be justified by their earnings prospects. Some observers were concerned that the high stock prices were part of a "bubble" that was doomed to burst. In December 1996, long before stock prices ultimately stopped rising, Federal Reserve Chairman Alan Greenspan remarked that the prices people were willing to pay for stocks reflected "irrational exuberance" on the part of financial investors. In March 2000, these concerns appeared to be justified, as stock prices—particularly technology stock prices—began to fall. Just as the NASDAQ had increased much more sharply than the S&P 500 index during the stock price boom, it fell much more precipitously during the crash. Within a year after reaching its peak, the NASDAQ index had lost 60% of its value, to the dismay of those who had put their savings in technology stock shares.

What were the macroeconomic effects of the boom and bust in stock prices? We have emphasized two major macroeconomic channels for stock prices: a wealth effect on consumption and an effect on capital investment through Tobin's q. The *wealth effect* on consumption arises because stocks are a component of households' financial assets, which in turn contribute to households' present value of lifetime resources (PVLR). Because a stock market boom makes households better off financially, they should respond by consuming more; and likewise, a bust in the stock market reduces household wealth and should reduce consumption. The Application "The Response of Consumption to Stock Market Crashes and Booms" (pp. 116–118 of the Fourth Edition) discusses the role of the rising stock market in increasing consumption during the 1990s. That Application concludes that, empirically, the increase in stock prices during the 1990s contributed to the rise in consumption, but that other factors appeared to be important as well. What about the effect on consumption of the subsequent stock market decline? Although stock prices fell for more than a year after peaking in March 2000, the ratio of real consumption to real GDP showed only a slight drop in the second quarter of 2000 and then rose steadily for each of the remaining quarters in 2000 and 2001. The wealth effect of the stock market on consumption was thus not evident in the aggregate data after the stock prices began to decline, although it should be kept in mind that the stocks that make up the NASDAQ index in particular account for a relatively small share of total household wealth.

The other channel by which the stock market can affect the aggregate demand for goods is through *Tobin's q*, which is discussed in Box 4.1, "Investment and the Stock Market" (p. 131).[1] Tobin's q is the ratio of the market value of firms to the replacement cost of their capital stocks. When Tobin's q is greater than one, it is profitable to acquire additional capital because the value of the capital exceeds the cost of acquiring it. More generally, the higher the value of Tobin's q, the greater the incentive for firms to invest in new capital. Figure 2 shows quarterly data on Tobin's q and real private nonresidential investment. Consistent with the theory, the two are closely related; Tobin's q and investment rose together throughout the

---

1. James Tobin of Yale University, the Nobel laureate who originated the concept of Tobin's q, died in March 2002.

Figure 2
Investment and Tobin's *q*
Sources: Investment data from
BEA Web site; *q* data from
www.valuingwallstreet.com,
Fed *q*, excluding land.

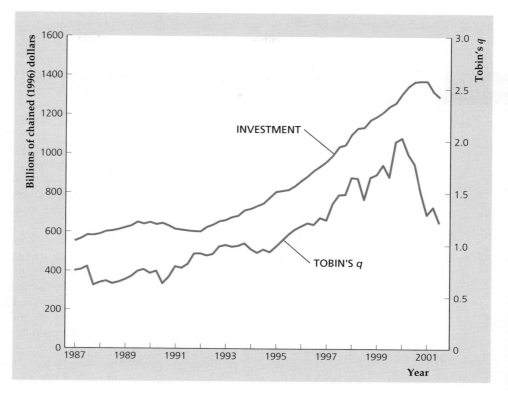

1990s and then both fell in 2000. Tobin's *q* reached its peak in the first quarter of 2000, when stock prices crested, and then fell substantially. With a delay of a few quarters, investment topped out and also fell, although not as sharply as Tobin's *q* fell. This behavior of investment appears quite consistent with the theory, especially when we take account of lags in the process of making investment decisions, planning capital formation, and implementing the plans.

A U.S. Productivity Miracle?

As described in Chapter 6, pp. 211–215, of the Fourth Edition, productivity growth in the United States slowed considerably after about 1973. Table 1 shows one measure of productivity growth, growth in output per hour of work in the nonfarm business sector (essentially, growth in average labor productivity). As you can see from the table, average labor productivity rose by more than 12% during the five-year period that ended in 1975 but then grew much more slowly over the ensuing twenty years.

However, the table also shows that productivity growth rose sharply in the second half of the 1990s. Indeed, the 13.4% total increase in output per hour of work over the period 1995–2000 was nearly double the average rate in the four previous five-year periods. Rapid productivity growth contributed to the exceptionally strong economic performance of the late nineties. Real GDP and real wages grew rapidly, unemployment fell, stock prices soared, and the government's budget showed a healthy surplus, reflecting the high tax revenues generated by a booming economy.

Why did U.S. productivity growth increase so markedly in the latter part of the 1990s? Economic research suggests that much of the speedup can be traced, directly or indirectly, to the revolution in information and communications technologies (ICT) that gathered steam in the 1990s.[1] First, computers and other high-tech equipment improved even more rapidly after 1995 than in previous years, showing major gains in processing speeds, memory, and other features. For example, according to "Moore's Law," first stated by Gordon Moore in 1965, the number of transistors that can fit on a chip (and hence computer processing speeds) can be expected to double every eighteen months; apparently, the time required for doubling computational speed dropped from 18 months to about 12 months during the post-1995 period.[2] These technical improvements were reflected in higher measured productivity in the sectors producing computers and other high-tech equipment—a direct impact on the productivity statistics.

Second, more indirectly, firms responded to the increased marginal product of high-tech capital by investing heavily in computers, software, and communications equipment. Indeed, nearly half of all U.S. investment in equipment in 2000 was in computers and software. These investments in new technologies helped to raise the productivity of workers using the new equipment.

---

1. For an overview of this research see Robert J. Gordon, "Technology and Economic Performance in the American Economy," National Bureau of Economic Research, Working Paper 8771, February 2002. Also see Dale W. Jorgenson and Kevin J. Stiroh, "Raising the Speed Limit: U.S. Economic Growth in the Information Age," *Brookings Papers on Economic Activity*, 31:1, 2000, pp. 125–211, and Stephen D. Oliner and Daniel E. Sichel, "The Resurgence of Growth in the Late 1990s: Is Information Technology the Story?" *Journal of Economic Perspectives*, Fall 2000, pp. 3–22.

2. Gordon (2002), op. cit., p. 22.

Table 1

Growth In Average Labor Productivity

Period	Total Productivity Growth
1970–1975	12.3 %
1975–1980	5.9
1980–1985	8.9
1985–1990	6.7
1990–1995	7.9
1995–2000	13.4

Source: Economic Report of the President, February 2002, Table B-49 (output per hour of all persons, nonfarm business sector), p. 378; and authors' calculations.

Third, technological developments in ICT may have been transplanted to other industries, boosting technological progress in these other sectors as well. For example, advances in computer technology have helped automotive engineers design more gas-efficient and more powerful cars. However, most of these technological "spillover" effects appear to have occurred in industries producing durable goods, such as automobiles, machinery, and airplanes, and less so in other parts of the economy, such as the service sector.

A question of crucial importance is whether the higher rate of productivity growth observed in recent years will continue, stimulating further economic growth. It seems unlikely to many observers that technological progress in the ICT sector can continue at the rapid rate seen in recent years; if it does not, the direct contribution of the ICT sector to aggregate productivity growth will decline. However, there are also some grounds for optimism. A first hopeful sign is that productivity growth continued through the recession that began in March 2001, contrary to the usual finding that productivity slows significantly or even declines during recessions. Second, and much more significant for the longer run, a number of economists and industrial leaders have argued that the productivity benefits of improved technologies have only begun to spread through the broader economy. If this viewpoint is correct, then even if technological progress in the production of computers slows, we should continue to see substantial productivity growth in industries that use computers and other high-tech equipment.

U.S. Monetary Aggregates, 2002

Monetary aggregates are alternative measures of the amount of money in the U.S. economy. Although (for reasons discussed in Chapter 14) monetary aggregates play a smaller role in monetary policymaking today than in the past, many economists still find monetary aggregates to be useful indicators of monetary policy and the general state of the economy.

Table 1 gives recent data for U.S. monetary aggregates. Comparing this table to the version on p. 245 of the Fourth Edition, which presents similar monetary data for July 1999, you will notice some important changes in the composition of the monetary aggregates. Currency held by the public grew by 20% over the two and a half years ending in January 2002. This large increase in currency in the hands of the public may reflect a rising demand for dollars overseas. (See Box 7.2 of the Fourth Edition, "Where Have All the Dollars Gone?," p. 247. The Chapter 13 *UPDATE* explains why overseas holders of other currencies, notably the German mark, may have chosen to switch to dollars during 1999–2002.) Over this same period, holdings of demand deposits actually fell, with about two-thirds of this decline appearing as an increase in other checkable deposits. Over the past thirty years, other checkable deposits—which, unlike demand deposits, pay interest—have grown dramatically relative to demand deposits.

Americans also greatly increased their holdings of savings deposits between July 1999 and January 2002, perhaps in search of greater security in the face of uncertainty in financial markets and the economy. Increased savings deposits in turn contributed to an almost 20% increase in M2, and a large associated decline in M2 velocity from 2.02 at the end of the second quarter of 1999 to 1.87 at the end of 2001. Thus M2 velocity, which has varied considerably less than M1 velocity in the past (see Figure 7.1, p. 258 of the Fourth Edition), has recently proved to be fairly unstable.

Table 1 (Table 7.1 updated)

U.S. Monetary Aggregates (January 2002)

M1	**1184.3**
Currency	584.4
Travelers' checks	8.0
Demand deposits	329.0
Other checkable deposits	262.9
M2	**5477.5**
Components of M1	1184.3
Savings deposits, including MMDAs	2336.7
Small-denomination time deposits	961.1
MMMFs (noninstitutional)	995.3

Note: Numbers may not add to totals due to rounding.
Source: http://www.stls.frb.org/fred/data/monetary.html. Data are not seasonally adjusted.

Dating the Peak of the 2001 Recession

The beginning of a recession is called a *peak* because it represents the high point of economic activity prior to a downturn. The end of a recession, which marks the low point of economic activity, is called the recession's *trough* (Chapter 8, pp. 275–276, in the Fourth Edition). For many years, the dates of peaks and troughs have been determined by the National Bureau of Economic Research (NBER), a nonprofit organization that supports a wide variety of applied research in economics. The NBER has also dated recessions retrospectively back to 1854 (Table 8.1, p. 279 in the Fourth Edition).

As of the beginning of 2001, there had been no "official" recession in the United States since the one that began in July 1990 and ended in March 1991. The ten-year span without a recession was the longest in U.S. history. Indeed, the period from 1982 until 2001, referred to as the "long boom," was probably the most recession-free in U.S. history, including a total of only eight months of contraction. However, the economy weakened considerably during the latter part of 2000 and in the spring and summer of 2001. A further blow was the terrorist attacks of September 11, 2001, which caused significant job losses in New York City and (because people became afraid to travel) in industries such as airlines and hotels. Because of the increased likelihood that a recession had begun, the six economists who form the Business Cycle Dating Committee—the group within the NBER that "calls" recession dates—convened in November 2001.

Determining whether a recession had begun in 2001, and if so, in which month the peak occurred, posed an unusually difficult task for the NBER committee. The committee relies heavily on a number of monthly statistical indicators that provide information about the state of the economy. Four of the most important indicators are

- industrial production, which measures the output of factories and mines;
- sales in manufacturing and trade (both wholesale and retail);
- nonfarm employment; and
- real personal income (excluding transfers such as Social Security payments)

Each of these indicators measures a different aspect of the economy. Because their movements tend to coincide with the overall movements in the economy, they are called *coincident indicators*.

Unfortunately, from the perspective of trying to fix a date for the peak, the four major coincident indicators—which normally move more or less together—were less synchronized than usual in 2000 and 2001. Industrial production (see Figure 1) and sales in manufacturing and trade had begun to decline significantly as early as September 2000. This slump in manufacturing reflected slow sales of information technology (computers, software, communications devices, and so on) following the collapse of the "dot-com bubble" beginning in March 2000. (The values of many high-tech stocks had fallen by two-thirds or more during the year.) However,

Figure 1
**Industrial production,
January 2000–January
2002**
The chart shows monthly
values for the industrial
production index for the
period January
2000–January 2002.
Compare to Figure 8.2, p.
289 of the Fourth Edition.
Source: Board of Governors of
the Federal Reserve. Available
online at
http://www.nber.org

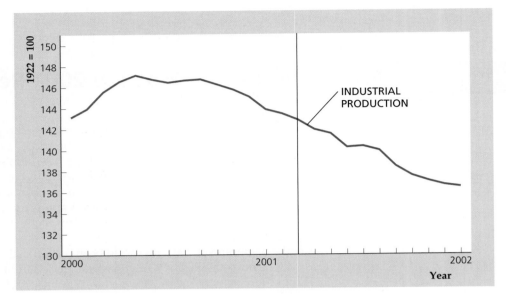

the weakness in manufacturing had not been immediately reflected in the economy as a whole, as both employment and real personal income had grown strong-
ly in the fall of 2000. Nonfarm employment did not start to decline until March 2001
(see Figure 2), and real personal income did not decline until October 2001.

After considering all the evidence, the NBER committee dated a recession peak
in March 2001. Based on employment and other indicators, March appeared to be
the month in which the weakness in the industrial sector of the previous fall was
finally felt more broadly in the economy. And although the recession did not

Figure 2
**Total nonfarm
employment, January
2000–January 2002**
The chart shows monthly
values for total nonfarm
employment, in millions,
for the period January
2000–January 2002.
Compare to Figure 8.4, p.
290 of the Fourth Edition,
which shows a very simi-
lar but not quite identical
variable.
Source: Bureau of Labor
Statistics. Available online at
http://www.nber.org

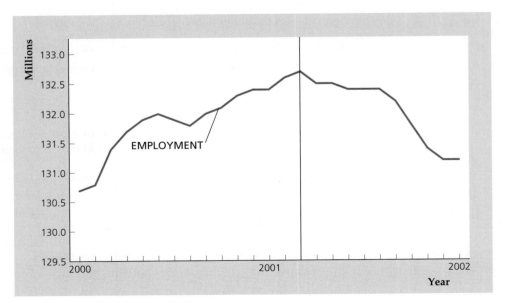

appear to be an unusually deep one by historical standards, by the end of 2001 it was clear that economic activity had fallen significantly. For example, between March 2001 and December 2001, total nonfarm employment fell by 1.4 million jobs, about the same in percentage terms as in six previous recessions.

For more information on how the NBER measures recessions and establishes peak and trough dates, see http://www.nber.org/cycles/recessions.html.

•

Efficiency Wages in the Laboratory: Testing Akerlof's Gift-Exchange Theory

The 2001 Nobel Prize in Economic Science was awarded to three American economists—George Akerlof, Michael Spence, and Joseph Stiglitz—each of whom did pioneering research on the implications of *incomplete* or *imperfect information* for economic performance. In a variety of applications, these three economists showed that missing or inaccurate information can lead markets to perform quite inefficiently, in contrast to the *invisible hand* theory (p. 17 of the Fourth Edition), which holds that markets generally do a good job of allocating resources.

One market for which incomplete information is potentially very important is the labor market. In the market for apples, for example, buyers can observe fairly accurately the quality of the product being offered for sale. In the market for labor, by contrast, purchasers of labor (employers) may find it difficult to judge the skill or motivation of the workers they hire, or to monitor the effort that workers put into their jobs. A consequence of these informational problems is that employers may choose to pay wages above the market-clearing level, in the hope of attracting better workers, reducing turnover, or eliciting greater effort. The idea that firms may find it profitable to pay above-market-clearing wages is the *efficiency wage theory*, discussed in Chapter 11 of the Fourth Edition.

The version of the efficiency wage theory discussed in the text emphasizes the effect of higher real wages on worker effort. Why might workers who are better paid put forth more effort? One explanation, suggested by Nobelist George Akerlof, is that employees are motivated to work harder for employers who treat them "fairly"— what Akerlof called the *gift exchange motive* (see p. 392 of the Fourth Edition).

Is the gift exchange motive important empirically? Questions of this type are often difficult to answer in real-life labor markets, because many factors are likely to influence worker effort and performance in practice, among them differences in workers' abilities and career aspirations. To complement research on real-world labor markets, some economists have set up and studied "artificial" labor markets in the laboratory, using human subjects. Although there is always the concern that people will behave differently in artificial laboratory settings than they do in real life, experiments have the important advantage of allowing the researcher to control more completely for possible influences on behavior outside those being studied.

Akerlof's gift-exchange hypothesis was the focus of a pioneering laboratory experiment by a trio of Austrian economists: Ernst Fehr, Georg Kirchsteiger, and Arno Riedl.[1] In their experiment, volunteers were randomly assigned to the roles of "employers" or "workers." The experiment itself had two stages. In the first

---

1. Ernst Fehr, Georg Kirchsteiger, and Arno Riedl, "Does Fairness Prevent Market Clearing? An Experimental Investigation," *Quarterly Journal of Economics*, 108, May 1993, 437–459.

stage, lasting three minutes, each "employer" anonymously entered into a computer the wage he or she was willing to pay. "Workers," receiving this information on their own computer screens, then decided whether or not to accept specific wages that were offered. Employers were allowed to "hire" more than one worker, but workers could choose at most one employer. Employers who were unable to hire workers were allowed to change their wage offers if they wished. At the end of this stage, employers were told how many workers had accepted their wage offers but not specifically which individuals had accepted them. Likewise, workers did not learn the identities of their employers.

The second stage of the experiment was intended to correspond to time on the job. In this stage, workers who had found an employer were asked to choose (secretly) a number between zero and one to represent their "effort" on the job—higher values representing higher effort. Anonymity was maintained; no one was told the identities of their respective employers or employees.

The researchers ran this experiment many times for each group of subjects. At the end of the session, participants received (actual) monetary rewards, based on their choices and actions during the rounds of the experiment. The monetary rewards of subjects playing the role of employers were reduced by the amounts they had paid in wages but were increased if "their" workers had offered high levels of effort. Workers, on the other hand, received monetary rewards that increased with the wage rates they had accepted but were reduced proportionally to the effort levels they had chosen (reflecting the reality that putting forth effort is costly).

According to standard economic analysis, there would be no reason for the people playing workers in this experiment to put forth more than the minimal possible effort. By the time they chose their effort levels, their wage had already been determined and would not be affected by their effort. Moreover, because the effort decisions were anonymous, employers could not retaliate in any way (either during or after the experiment) against specific workers who did not provide effort. Nevertheless, the authors reported that workers routinely provided considerably more than the minimal amount of effort in the second stage of the experiment; and that the amount of effort provided was higher, the higher the wage being received. (See Table 1.) The

Table 1
The Wage–Effort Relationship

Wage Received	Average Observed Effort Level
30–44	0.17
45–59	0.18
60–74	0.34
75–89	0.45
90–110	0.52

For the laboratory experiment described, the table shows the relationship between the wage that workers received (left column) and the effort that they put forth (right column). Effort is measured on a scale from zero to one. Note that the workers receiving the highest wages (in the range 90 to 110) exerted three times as much effort as workers receiving the lowest wages (30–44).

Source: Fehr, Kirchsteiger, and Riedl (1993), Table II, p. 446.

authors interpreted this behavior as an attempt by workers to reciprocate generous wage offers with generous behavior of their own. Moreover, in apparent anticipation of this response, employers offered wages higher than the minimum necessary to hire workers. Thus, in a laboratory setting at least, the idea that "workers" are willing to reward "employers" who pay them better wages seems to be borne out.

The Weakness of the Euro

On January 1, 1999, twelve European nations introduced a common currency, the euro. (See the Application, "European Monetary Unification," p. 510 of the Fourth Edition.) Actually, the euro made its debut in two phases. In the first phase, lasting three years, it was agreed that the euro would be a "virtual currency"; that is, there would be no actual euro notes or coins in circulation. Instead, people would continue to use the traditional currencies of Europe (such as German marks and French francs) in hand-to-hand circulation. In the second phase, beginning January 1, 2002, euro notes and coins would be introduced into circulation and the various national currencies would be phased out.

During the first, "virtual-currency" phase, with no actual euros in circulation, the value of a euro could be defined only in relation to the values of existing national currencies. Specifically, the twelve nations agreed to give meaning to the idea of a euro by establishing a permanent rate of exchange between the euro and each existing European currency. Some of these official rates of exchange are given below:

$$
\begin{aligned}
1 \text{ euro} \ &= \ 40.3399 \text{ Belgian francs} \\
&= \ 6.5596 \text{ French francs} \\
&= \ 1.95583 \text{ German marks} \\
&= 1936.27 \text{ Italian lire} \\
&= \ 166.386 \text{ Spanish pesetas}
\end{aligned}
$$

A key advantage of fixing the values of national currencies in terms of euros was that prices could be quoted anywhere in the participating countries in terms of euros as well as in the local currency, facilitating trade and economic integration. (Here is a rare situation in which the "medium of exchange" function of money might be served by one currency—the franc or the mark—and the "unit of account" function served by another, the euro. See Chapter 7 of the Fourth Edition, p. 244.) Other advantages of the new system related to exchange rates. First, as of January 1, 1999, the exchange rates between any two currencies in the European monetary union were effectively fixed; for example, because 6.5596 French francs and 1.95583 German marks both equal one euro, then it must also be the case that 6.5596/1.95583 French francs, or 3.354 francs, equal one mark. Second, after the introduction of the euro, it was no longer necessary for each European currency to have a separate exchange rate with currencies outside the European monetary area, such as the U.S. dollar. Instead, knowing the exchange rate between the euro and the dollar was sufficient to know the exchange rate between each national currency and the dollar. (For example, suppose a dollar equals 1.10 euros. How many French francs does a dollar equal? Use the rates of exchange in the table above.)

When the euro was officially introduced in 1999, the market-determined value of the euro was 1 euro = $1.16 (U.S.) However, to the surprise of many Europeans, the value of the euro in foreign-exchange markets began to fall steadily (see Figure 1). By the time that euro coins and notes were introduced into circulation on January 1,

Figure 1
Value of the mark and the euro, 1996–2002
The chart shows the value, in terms of dollars, of the German mark and the euro. Data for the mark are shown for January 1996 through January 2002. Data for the euro begin with its introduction in January 1999. One euro equals 1.956 German marks. Notice that the value of the euro (and, consequently, the mark, which is tied to the euro) fell significantly after its introduction in January 1999.
Source: Federal Reserve Bank of St. Louis, http://www.stls.frb.org/fred/

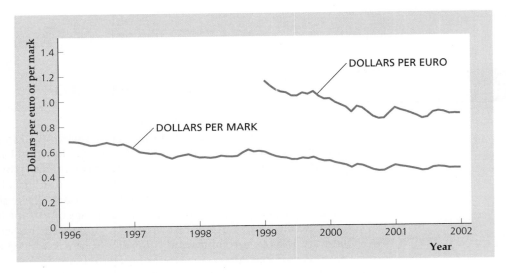

2002, the value of the euro had dropped to 1 euro = $0.89, that is, the euro had depreciated by nearly one-fourth relative to the dollar in only three years. The sharp fall in the euro drove up the cost of imports for Europeans (while making European vacations a great deal for American tourists!); and it proved a political embarrassment to the new European Central Bank, which had promised that the euro would be a "strong" currency.

Several explanations have been proposed for the euro's unexpected decline. One of these centers on the attractiveness of U.S. assets to European financial investors. At the time that the euro was introduced, the U.S. economy and stock market were booming, particularly in the high-tech sector. According to this explanation, Europeans were eager to invest in what they perceived to be high-yielding U.S. assets. In order to buy U.S. assets, European financial investors sold euros and bought dollars, driving down the value of the euro relative to the dollar. This explanation is consistent with the large financial inflows experienced by the United States during this period as well as with the strength of the dollar relative to virtually all currencies (not just the euro). However, if the booming U.S. economy and stock market were the whole story, the euro should have strengthened somewhat when the U.S. economy weakened and stock prices declined during the year 2000; but it did not.

An alternative explanation for the sinking euro has been offered by German economists Hans-Werner Sinn and Frank Westermann.[1] Sinn and Westermann pointed out that much of the demand for stable currencies, like the U.S. dollar and the German mark, comes from outside the countries that issue those currencies. In particular, dollars and marks—often stuffed in suitcases or in mattresses—have long proved to be attractive stores of value in countries experiencing high inflation or political instability (see Box 7.2, "Where Have All the Dollars Gone?," p. 247 of the Fourth Edition). While dollars have been particularly popular in Russia and Latin America, marks have been the currency of choice in many eastern European

---

1. "Why Has the Euro Been Falling? An Investigation into the Determinants of the Exchange Rate," National Bureau of Economic Research, Working Paper 8352, July 2001.

nations, especially after the fall of Communism, owing to their proximity to Germany. Indeed, Bosnia made the mark its official currency in August 1997.

According to Sinn and Westermann, the introduction of the euro in January 1999 posed a problem for foreign holders of marks. Hearing that the mark was to be abolished in favor of the euro, many holders of "black-market" marks outside Germany began to worry that their cash hoards might become worthless. More sophisticated holders of marks understood that their cash would be convertible into euros but were concerned that the conversion process would be difficult or might force them to reveal their mark holdings to the authorities. If it had been possible, many mark-holders might have traded their marks for euros on the black market; however, euros did not yet exist in physical form, making such unofficial transactions impossible! By Sinn and Westermann's account, mark-holders chose instead to sell their marks and obtain dollars, raising the value of the dollar and reducing the value of the mark. Because the mark was officially tied to the euro, the falling mark implied a falling euro as well, as you can see in the figure. Consistent with this story is a substantial increase in dollars in circulation during this period (see Chapter 7 *UPDATE*) and a corresponding decline in outstanding marks.

With the introduction of euro currency and coin into circulation in January 2002, it is now possible to hold hoards of cash in euros as easily as in dollars. Indeed, because euro notes come in relatively large denominations, euros may become more attractive than dollars for hoarding purposes. So, if the Sinn–Westermann story is correct, the euro should gradually strengthen as the demand for euro notes rises in eastern Europe and elsewhere.

Crisis in Argentina

On January 1, 2002, Eduardo Duhalde became Argentina's third president within two weeks, not counting several others who briefly held the office during transitions between governments. This political instability was the result of a deep recession, high unemployment, and a crushing international debt that led Argentines to take to the streets in large numbers to protest against the government. How did this all come about?

The Argentine story has been one of intermittent economic progress interrupted by periodic crises. During the 1970s and 1980s, Argentina's main economic problem was persistent, extreme inflation. By the fourth quarter of 1990, the CPI in Argentina was more than 10 billion times its level at the beginning of 1975! During the 1980s, Argentina twice changed its currency in unsuccessful attempts to halt its spectacularly high inflation. Shortly after Raul Alfonsin was elected President in December 1983, Argentina created a new "peso Argentino" equal to 10,000 old pesos. Less than two years later, in June 1985, Argentina introduced yet another new currency, the austral, declaring each austral the equivalent of 1,000 peso Argentinos. These changes in currencies were accompanied by other economic policy changes. However, neither attempt at stopping inflation proved successful.

A third attempt at curbing inflation, in April 1991, worked much better; indeed, following the 1991 policy changes, Argentina had virtually no inflation for more than a decade. One element of the 1991 anti-inflation policy was the creation of yet another new currency, called the new peso, worth 10,000 australs. Much more important than the new currency, however, was a comprehensive reform package, designed by Economics Minister Domingo Cavallo and supported by Argentine President Carlos Menem. Cavallo's package reduced the size of the government's budget deficit and introduced measures to make the Argentine economy more competitive internationally. The budget deficit was reduced by cutting back on public spending, reforming the tax system, and cracking down on tax evasion. To open up the Argentine economy to foreign competition, the government reduced tariffs and removed various restrictions on imports.

However, the linchpin of the successful 1991 reform was the so-called Convertibility Law, which established a *currency board* in Argentina. A currency board is a monetary arrangement under which the supply of domestic currency in circulation is strictly limited by the amount of foreign reserves held by the central bank. The purpose of a currency board is to impose discipline on the central bank. By limiting the central bank's power to create money, the currency board helps to reassure the public that the money supply will not be recklessly increased. A stable money supply in turn should ensure that domestic inflation will be held in check, and that the nominal exchange rate can be maintained at a constant value.

Specifically, under the 1991 Convertibility Law, the exchange rate for Argentina's new peso was fixed at one U.S. dollar per peso, and the law limited the total number of pesos in circulation to no more than the number of U.S. dollars held by the Argentine central bank. (In practice, some loopholes in the law allowed dollar holdings to be a bit lower than pesos in circulation.) Because Argentine pesos were supposed to be fully backed, one-for-one, by U.S. dollars, the currency board gave holders of pesos confidence that their pesos could be easily and quickly converted into dollars—and, hence, that "a peso is as good as a dollar."

The establishment of the currency board and the other reforms implemented by Cavallo in 1991 seemed to be very successful. The currency board achieved its goal of price stability. During the second half of the 1990s, the Argentine inflation rate was essentially zero—indeed, the CPI in the fourth quarter of 1999 was slightly lower than in the fourth quarter of 1995. The real economy also performed well for much of the 1990s: Real GDP grew at an average rate of 5.8% per year from 1990 to 1998, an impressive rate that appears even more impressive when compared to the –0.2% per year average growth rate in Argentina from 1975 to 1990. By the mid 1990s, the 1991 reform package was widely viewed as a resounding success.

In the latter part of the 1990s, however, Argentina slipped into recession, with real GDP falling by 3.4% in 1999 and the unemployment rate rising well into double digits. Moreover, other economic clouds loomed on the horizon. Government budget deficits, a traditional problem in Argentina, grew again, reflecting attempts to stimulate the economy through increased spending, higher wages for government workers, and the large costs incurred in a major reform of the social security system. With a rapidly increasing need to borrow, the government found the public unwilling to buy government debt, and so it raised funds by coercing private commercial banks into making loans to the government. Depositors, alarmed that these forced loans might threaten the financial health of the banks, began to withdraw their funds. To slow the outflow of deposits from banks, on December 1, 2001, the government imposed a *corralito* (fence) that limited withdrawals by depositors to $1000 per month. Although the measure reduced withdrawals of deposits, it also severely disrupted commerce.

In addition to its domestic fiscal problems, Argentina suffered from an increasingly overvalued real exchange rate (see Figure 13.11, p. 501 of the Fourth Edition), particularly in comparison with trading partners such as Brazil. In January 1999 the Brazilian *real* depreciated by almost 40% relative to the U.S. dollar and the Argentine peso. This 40% increase in the value of the peso relative to the *real* sharply increased the real exchange rate of the peso and further exacerbated Argentina's current account problems. Moreover, because the U.S. dollar was quite strong during this period, the peso's one-for-one link to the dollar implied that the peso would be strong as well.

Throughout most of the 1990s, Argentina ran large current account deficits, leading its foreign debt to grow to about one-half of a year's GDP. One response to an overvalued fixed exchange rate is to devalue, bringing its official value closer to its fundamental value. In Argentina's case, a lower exchange rate might have also helped its current account deficit, by stimulating exports and restraining imports. However, the currency board arrangement in Argentina, which maintained Argentina's exchange rate fixed in terms of the dollar, did not permit an easy devaluation. Argentina was reluctant to devalue the peso because it did not want to undermine the currency board that was widely viewed as the source of price stability.

But the deepening recession, the heavy interest payments on foreign debt, and the riots in the streets took their toll. Argentina announced that it would cease payment on its $155 billion of foreign debt, the largest such default in history. Then, in January 2002, Argentina abandoned the currency board and let the nominal value of the peso float relative to the dollar. On January 10, 2002, the peso lost 29% of its value, falling from one dollar per peso to only 0.713 dollars per peso. By February 1, the peso had lost fully half of its value, selling at a price of 0.494 dollars. Halving the value of the peso doubled the number of pesos needed to pay any dollar amount of debt owed to foreigners. This sudden doubling in the peso value of dollar-denominated foreign debt forced many borrowers to default on loans. It remains to be seen when, and whether, the sharp devaluation will substantially improve Argentina's current account balance, or whether Argentina can stabilize its economy without reigniting inflation.

The Federal Reserve Responds to the Recession

As discussed in the Chapter 8 *UPDATE,* the U.S. industrial sector began to slow in the fall of 2000, and the broader economy weakened in subsequent months. The National Bureau of Economic Research declared that a recession had begun in March 2001.

At the end of 2000, the Federal funds rate, the interest rate that is the Fed's principal instrument of monetary policy, stood at 6.50%. The Fed cut the rate sharply in January 2001 and then continued to cut throughout the year as evidence mounted of an economic slowdown. The Fed also eased monetary policy in response to the shock waves created by the terrorist attacks of September 11, 2001. By January 2002, the Federal funds rate had been cut by nearly five full percentage points, all the way to 1.75%, (see Figure 1). By slashing interest rates, the Fed hoped to stimulate spending on investment and consumption. Consumer spending, including spending on durable goods such as automobiles, remained fairly strong through 2001, but investment remained weak.

An important limitation on the power of monetary policy is that the Fed directly influences only very short-term interest rates like the Federal funds rate. However, many spending decisions, such as home purchases, require long-term loans and thus are more sensitive to long-term interest rates than to short-term interest rates. Because long-term interest rates are determined by expectations of

Figure 1
The Federal Funds Rate and the Ten-Year Bond Rate
The chart shows monthly values for the Federal funds rate and the ten-year Treasury bond rate for the period January 2000–February 2002. Compare to Figure 14.5, p. 538 of the Fourth Edition.
Source: H.15 release of the Board of Governors of the Federal Reserve. Available online at http://www.stls.frb.org/fred/fredfile.html#interest

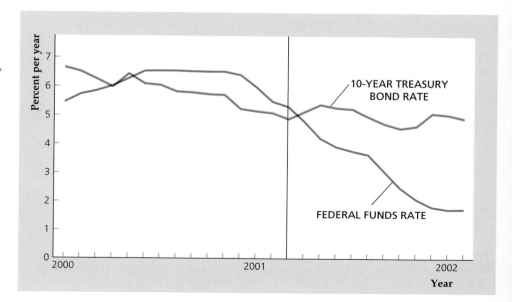

inflation and the real interest rate over a long period (ten years or more), they respond less dramatically to short-run changes in monetary policy. Figure 1 contrasts the behavior of the ten-year Treasury bond rate (the interest rate paid by the government for funds that it borrows for ten years from the public) with the Federal funds rate. You can see that, although it declined somewhat, the long-term bond rate fell by much less than the Federal funds rate did during the period. (See "In Touch with the Macroeconomy: Interest Rates," p. 121 of the Fourth Edition, for further discussion of short-term versus long-term interest rates.)

Game Theory Goes to the Oscars

In March 2002 the movie "A Beautiful Mind" won the coveted Academy Award (the "Oscar") for Best Picture of the Year. Ron Howard also won an Oscar for his work as director of the film. "A Beautiful Mind" was loosely based on Sylvia Nasar's best-selling biography of John Nash, a mathematician who has fought a courageous, lifelong battle against mental illness. The movie's climax comes with Nash's acceptance of the Nobel Prize in Economics, which he received for his important early work in game theory, a branch of mathematics that has had wide application in economics.

John Nash's major contribution to game theory was his analysis of a concept that has come to be known as Nash equilibrium. A *Nash equilibrium* is the outcome of a game (or other strategic situation) in which each player takes the action most favorable for herself, under the assumption that other players will (independently) do the same. In effect, Nash studied the outcomes of games in which explicit agreement or cooperation among players is ruled out, and each person just does the best that she can for herself.

Chapter 14 of the Fourth Edition shows how game theory can be used to analyze the concept of central bank credibility (see pp. 548–554). The examples we give there make implicit use of the concept of Nash equilibrium. For example, look again at the game between Dad and the kids (Figure 14.8, p. 549). The kids, who "move" first in the game, choose to fight or not to fight. In making their choice, they do the best they can for themselves, under the assumption that Dad will do the same when it becomes his turn to move. The outcome of the game when both players independently choose their best action—the game's Nash equilibrium—is described by cell A (kids fight but get to go to the game). As discussed in the text, the Nash equilibrium of this game yields an outcome that is less desirable (for Dad, at least) than cell B, in which the kids don't fight and everyone gets to go to the game. In general, as John Nash first showed, the Nash equilibrium of a game may not be the best outcome for all the players in the game. Often, cooperation or coordination among players in a game or other strategic situation can yield a better outcome for everyone than the Nash equilibrium outcome, in which everyone acts independently. (See Figure 14.8, p. 552 of the Fourth Edition for an example.)